CHARACTERS

JASPER FEATHERWAYS	. . . *Noel Coward.*
JANE (his Wife)	. *Gertrude Lawrence.*
LAVINIA FEATHERWAYS	. . . *Alison Leggatt.*
RICHARD FEATHERWAYS	. . . *Edward Underdown.*
HARRIET WINTER .	. . . *Everley Gregg.*
CHARLES WINTER .	. . . *Anthony Pelissier.*
EMILY VALANCE .	. . . *Moya Nugent.*
EDWARD VALANCE .	. . . *Kenneth Carten.*
BURROWS . . .	. . . *Alan Webb.*

The action of the play passes in the drawing-room of the Featherways' house in Kent on an Autumn evening in the year 1860.

FAMILY ALBUM

The scene is the drawing-room of the Featherways' house in Kent, not very far from London.

It is an Autumn evening in the year 1860.

(See Photograph of Scene.)

When the CURTAIN *rises the entire family is assembled. They are all in deep mourning. The music plays softly; an undercurrent to grief.* EMILY *is by the window;* RICHARD *is slightly up* L. *of her;* LAVINIA *is seated at* R. *end of the couch;* JASPER *is standing in front of the fireplace;* JANE *is sitting on the downstage seat* C; HARRIET *is sitting on the upstage seat* C.; CHARLES *is leaning against the pillar at the back of the couch;* EDWARD *is standing and leaning with one hand on the* L. *side of the pillar up* R.C.

The family group would be static were it not for an occasional slight movement from one or other of them. Apart from the music there is silence for quite a while. EMILY *breaks it.*

EMILY. It has stopped raining.

RICHARD (*moving to the window*). Not quite, Emily, but it is certainly clearing.

LAVINIA. It was fitting that it rained to-day. It has been a sad day and rain became it.

JASPER. True, very true.

JANE. A little sunshine would have been much pleasanter nevertheless.

JASPER. Lavinia has a tidy mind. She likes life to be as neat as her handkerchief drawer.

HARRIET. I hope Mr. Lubbock reached London safely.

JANE. Dear Mr. Lubbock!

7

LAVINIA. Really, Jane!

JANE. I think he's a sweet man. He read the will with such sympathy.

HARRIET. He coughed a great deal, I thought. I wanted to give him one of my pastilles.

CHARLES. I'm glad you didn't, my dear, they have an alarming flavour and he was already considerably nervous.

HARRIET. They're very efficacious.

EMILY (*pensively—at the window*). I wonder if he knew.

EDWARD. What was that, my love?

EMILY. Papa—I wonder if he knew it was raining?

LAVINIA. Perhaps he was watching—from somewhere above the trees.

HARRIET. Oh! Do you suppose he was?

LAVINIA. I like to think it.

JANE. Do you, Lavinia?

LAVINIA. Of course.

JANE. When I die I hope I shall go swiftly and not linger above familiar trees. It must be painful to watch those you have left, in black and weeping.

EMILY. Oh, don't, Jane, don't! (*She weeps, and sits in the armchair* R.C.)

EDWARD (*comforting her*). There, there, my dear.

HARRIET. Poor Papa!

EMILY. Poor dear Papa!

(*The door opens quietly and* BURROWS, *a very aged butler, enters staggering under the weight of a heavy tray on which is a decanter containing Madeira, and the requisite number of glasses.* RICHARD *goes quickly and relieves him of it and puts it on the table* R.C.)

RICHARD. Oh, Burrows, you should have let Martin carry the tray, it's too heavy for you.

BURROWS (*cupping his ear with his hand*). Pardon, Master Richard?

JASPER (*who has crossed to* BURROWS—*bending down to him and speaking clearly*). You should have let Martin carry the tray, Burrows, it's too heavy for you.

BURROWS. Martin is young, Mr. Jasper. He would have been out of tune with the evening's melancholy. His very bearing would have been an intrusion.

LAVINIA. Thank you, Burrows, that was very considerate of you.

BURROWS. I beg your pardon, Miss Lavvy?

LAVINIA (*loudly*). I said thank you, Burrows, that was very considerate of you.

BURROWS. Your servant to the grave, Miss Lavvy.

JANE. Oh, Burrows!

BURROWS. I beg your pardon, Ma'am?

JANE (*loudly*). I only said " Oh, Burrows," Burrows.

BURROWS. Very good, Ma'am.

(BURROWS *goes out.* JASPER *has returned to the fireplace.*)

HARRIET. Poor Burrows looks very depressed.

JASPER. Burrows has looked depressed for at least thirty years.

JANE. One could scarcely expect him to be hilarious now.

LAVINIA. Hilarious! Really, Jane!

HARRIET. I think sorrow has increased his deafness.

JASPER. He was just as deaf last Christmas really, and that was a gay occasion.

JANE (*with meaning*). Gay!

JASPER (*reprovingly*). Hush, Jane.

HARRIET. A bereavement in the house must affect the servants profoundly, although I must admit I heard Sarah singing in the pantry this morning.

EMILY (*horrified—rising and crossing to* R. *of the couch*). This morning!

HARRIET. It was quite early.

LAVINIA. Disgraceful!

HARRIET. She was singing very softly, and it was a hymn.

LAVINIA. Nevertheless, I hope you scolded her.

HARRIET. I hadn't the heart, she has such a pretty voice.

CHARLES. What hymn was it?

HARRIET. " For those in peril on the sea."

LAVINIA. Most inappropriate.

JASPER. Sarah's young man is a sailor, you know, he's in the " Brilliant."

CHARLES (*with interest*). That's a Three-Decker.

EDWARD (*moving* C.). Yes. She carries one hundred and fourteen thirty-two pounders (*moves up to* RICHARD), two sixty-eight pounders and four eighteen pounders.

EMILY. Oh, Edward, how clever of you to know.

RICHARD. A fine ship, I have seen her at anchor.

CHARLES. Surely not a hundred and twenty guns ? (*He moves to* RICHARD *and* EDWARD.)

EDWARD. Yes, she is the same class as the " Britannic " and the " Prince Regent."

RICHARD. Cast-iron muzzle-loaders, I presume ?

EDWARD (*enthusiastically*). Yes, their recoil is checked by stout rope breechings.

CHARLES. How are they elevated ?

EDWARD. Quoins—and trained by handspikes.

RICHARD. Oh—handspikes.

JANE (*with slight mockery*). Handspikes, Lavinia—do you hear that ?—they're trained by handspikes !

LAVINIA. I declare I'm more at sea than Sarah's young man.

JANE. Oh, Lavvy—a joke—how sweet !

(EMILY *sits* L. *of* LAVINIA *on the couch.*)

EMILY (*hugging her*). Darling Lavvy !

LAVINIA. Behave, Emily—let me alone.

JASPER. It seems odd that the solemnity of this particular family reunion should be dissipated by gunnery.

LAVINIA. Such irrelevance, on such a day.

EDWARD. It was my fault, I apologize.

JANE. With so much to be done, so much to be decided.

LAVINIA (*raising her handkerchief to her eyes*). Oh, dear !

JASPER. Steel yourself, Lavinia—be brave.

LAVINIA. I'll try.

HARRIET. We must all try. (*She rises and moves* R.)

(CHARLES *and* RICHARD *go to the table on which* RICHARD *has placed the tray.*)

CHARLES. Jane—a little wine ?

JANE. Thank you, Charles.

CHARLES. Harriet ?

HARRIET. Thank you, Charles.

RICHARD. A little Madeira, Emily ?

EMILY. Just a drop, please.

RICHARD. Lavinia ?

LAVINIA. No, thank you.

HARRIET. Oh, Lavvy, a little sip would warm you

LAVINIA. I am not cold.

(EDWARD *hands wine to* HARRIET *and* JANE.)

JASPER (*brusquely*). Come, Lavvy, don't be annoying.

LAVINIA. How can you, Jasper——

JASPER. I insist—here—— (*He gives her a glass.*)

JANE. We should drink a toast.

LAVINIA. You should be ashamed.

JANE. Don't be alarmed, I meant quite a gentle toast.

RICHARD. An excellent idea.

CHARLES. Why not ?

LAVINIA. As though this were a moment for celebrating.

CHARLES. Again—why not ? (*Handing wine to* JASPER.)

JASPER (*sternly*). Charles—behave yourself !

JANE. Charles is right. Why not indeed !

LAVINIA. I am at a loss to understand your behaviour this evening, Jane.

JANE. A billiard-room—I heard Charles and Harriet discussing it—they're going to have a billiard-room——

HARRIET. It's an extravagance—I told Charles it was an extravagance.

JANE. Never mind, you can afford it now.

CHARLES. That's what I say. (*He takes a glass to* EDWARD *and then returns to the table.*)

JANE. Isn't it splendid !—Isn't it absolutely splendid ?

LAVINIA (*immeasurably shocked*). What !

JANE. About Charles and Harriet being able to afford a billiard-room, about Emily and Edward being able to send John and Curly to Eton, about you, Lavinia, being able to buy a little house anywhere you like, about Jasper and me living here——

RICHARD (*above the table* R.C.). What about me ?

JASPER. I think Crockford's should be congratulated —that's where all your money goes.

RICHARD. Touché, Jasper—a new black fleece though, for the blackest of black sheep.

EMILY. Where will you go, Lavvy ?

LAVINIA. I feel this conversation to be abominably out of place.

(JANE *rises, puts down her glass and crosses to the couch in front of* LAVINIA *and kneels.*)

JASPER. Think, Lavvy—a little house in some gay country—France or Italy—you've always loved for-eigners—a little villa in the sun—you can paint your pictures—blue seas and cypresses—you could take tabby with you, she's an insular cat, but I doubt whether French or Italian mice taste so very different——

JANE. We'll all come and stay with you, Lavinia.

RICHARD (*crossing to* R. *of couch*). Hurrah, Lavinia —smile and say Hurrah !

LAVINIA (*struggling*). No—no——

(HARRIET *rises and moves over* L.)

EMILY. Yes—yes——

LAVINIA. Be still, Emily—for shame !

HARRIET. Her mouth twitched—I saw it.

JASPER (*tickling the back of her neck*). Come along, Lavvy——

LAVINIA (*slapping his hand away*). How dare you, Jasper !

JANE. Think of Mrs. Hodgson's bonnet at the funeral—do you remember ?—I nudged you——

LAVINIA (*breaking at last into laughter*). Oh, dear—

how horrid you all are—I hate you—it was the most
ridiculous bonnet I ever saw—like a little black pie——
Oh, dear——

JASPER. Are your glasses charged?

(JANE *crosses to the armchair* R.C., *sits and picks up her
glass*.)

LAVINIA. No, Jasper, no—I don't approve——
JASPER (*raising his glass*). To Mrs. Hodgson's little
black pie!
ALL (*raising their glasses*). Mrs. Hodgson's little
black pie!
JASPER (*triumphantly, as* LAVINIA *drinks*). There!
Some more, quickly, Richard.

(LAVINIA *chokes—everyone gathers round her and pats her
on the back.* RICHARD, CHARLES, EDWARD *and*
JASPER *refill all the glasses*.)

LAVINIA. This is so wrong—so dreadfully wrong——
JASPER. Another toast—be prepared——

(*He crosses to the table.* RICHARD *also goes to the
table.*)

LAVINIA. Please, stop, Jasper—the servants will
hear.

(RICHARD *goes to* HARRIET *at the couch.*)

JASPER (*coming* C. *and raising his glass*). To ourselves,
a closely united family, and the dear strangers who
have joined us—I allude to you, Jane darling, and
Charles and Edward——
CHARLES. Does that mean that we three may not
drink?
JASPER. Certainly not—drink to yourselves—to
each other—and the happiness of us all.
CHARLES. Good!
HARRIET. Do be quiet, Charles.
JASPER. Where was I?
JANE. To the happiness of all of us.

" Drinking Song "

JASPER.   Here's a toast to each of us
            And all of us together,
            Here's a toast to happiness
            And reasonable pride,
            May our touch on life be lighter
            Than a seabird's feather,
            May all sorrows as we pass
            Politely step aside.

(They all drink.)

JANE (*singing*).   Jasper, my love, you ask for too much
I fear,
What if your hopes should never come true, my dear ?
Best be prepared for sorrow to stay
At least for a day,
At least for a day.
How can we find the wisdom you dream for us ?
There must be tears in Destiny's scheme for us ;
But if at last we're able to smile,
We'll prove it was all worth while !

JASPER.   A commonplace sentiment, my dear Jane—
worthy neither of you, nor the moment.

JANE.   Moments change so swiftly, my love.

EMILY.   I thought what Jane said was beautiful.

JANE.   Hush, Emily, Jasper's chiding merely means
that he would have liked to have thought of it himself.

RICHARD.   Get on with the toast, Jasper.

JASPER.   Where was I ?

JANE.   Gasping in the deeps of your own imagination,
my love.

JASPER (*singing*).   Now I drink to those of us who,
happily united,
Ornament our family and share our joy and pain.
Charles, my friend, and Edward too, connubially plighted,
Last, my dears, but always best, my own beloved Jane.

JANE (*spoken*).   Charmingly put, Jasper, if a trifle
pedantic.

JASPER.   I do my best, dear, but my best is obviously unworthy.

HARRIET.   Do stop sparring, you two.

LAVINIA.   Sparring! What a vulgar expression.

JASPER.   Where was I?

JANE.   In command, my love, as always.

(CHARLES *goes and stands with his back to the fire during the following.*)

JASPER (*singing*).   Harriet married a soldier,
  A man of pleasant birth,
  A man of sterling worth
  And finely-tempered steel,
  Ready to die for the Empire,
  The sun must never set
  Upon this brave but yet
  Ambiguous ideal.
  So now, dear Charles, I am saluting you,
  That never setting sun
  Shall call you blest,
  If far-off natives take to shooting you,
  You will at least have done
  Your level best.

ALL.   Harriet married a soldier,
  May life be bright for him,
  May might be right for him
  For ever and for aye.
  Harriet married a soldier,
  And in the matrimonial fray,
  Harriet married a soldier,
  Despite his glories in the field
  He'll have to honour and obey
  And be defeated 'til Judgment Day!

HARRIET (*spoken*).   How unfair of you all—I'm as meek as a mouse. Charles rules me with a rod of iron.

JANE.   Dear Harriet, we salute your strategy that makes him believe it.

(*All laugh.*)

JASPER (*singing*). Now we come to Emily, whose
    progress has been steady,
Only married two short years and three fat sons
already !

EMILY (*spoken*). You make me blush, Jasper—we
count the twins as one.

EDWARD. Nevertheless, my love, they are normal
babies with a mouth each to feed.

(EDWARD *moves down to* JASPER *during the following.*)

JASPER (*singing*).   Emily married a doctor,
                A mild and gentle man,
                A sentimental man
                Of scientific mind,
                Doing his best for the nation,
                For ever dutiful,
                A really beautiful
                Example for the rest of us,
                A challenge to the zest of us,
                The noblest and the best of us
                Combined.

EDWARD (*spoken*). I accept your tribute, Jasper,
while doubting its complete sincerity.

EMILY. Oh, Edward !

EDWARD. But the surface value is warming enough
—I thank you, Jasper.

(EDWARD *moves up.* JANE *takes off her scarf.*)

JASPER (*singing*). Now then, for my dearest dear
I must ask your kind and grave indulgence, for
How then can I make it clear to you ?

JANE. Sweet love, I appreciate—(*She rises and crosses
    to* JASPER.)
All these noble sentiments, but time is so
Fleet, love, what's this hesitating for——
Waiting for ?

JASPER. You, love,
For ever a part of me,
True love
Enshrined in the heart of me,

Who cares what dreams we may lose?
For ever we choose
This lovely illusion.
  JANE. After
The difficult years have fled,
Laughter
Will mock at the tears we've shed,
We hold the future in store
Together for evermore.
  ALL (*rising*). Here's a toast for each of them and
    both of them together,
Here's a toast to happiness and reasonable pride,
May their touch on life be lighter than a seabird's
    feather,
May their sorrows, as they pass, politely step aside.

(JANE *and* JASPER *walk round together during the chorus.
They drink. The gaiety is interrupted by the clock on
the mantelpiece striking ten. The music drops to the
minor. Everyone puts down his glass.*)

LAVINIA. Papa's eight-day clock—he would never
allow anyone to wind it but himself—who will wind it
now? (*She bows her head.*)

(EMILY, JASPER, HARRIET *and* RICHARD *all sing sadly
together.*)

EMILY.
JASPER.   ⎫ Ah, who will wind it now—alack-a-day—
HARRIET. ⎰   who will wind it now!
RICHARD.
JANE. Jasper, of course! (*She crosses* L.)
JASPER. Richard, be so kind as to ring for Burrows.
RICHARD (*crossing to the bell*). Now?
JASPER. Yes, now.
RICHARD. Very well.
LAVINIA (*now seated on the couch*). The box?
JASPER. The box.

  (RICHARD *pulls the bell-rope by the fireplace.*)

EMILY. Oh, dear!

(There is a gloomy silence for a moment. EDWARD breaks it.)

EDWARD (*at the window*). Look—there's a squirrel!

CHARLES (*eagerly, crossing to the window*). Where?

EDWARD. There—by the steps.

RICHARD (*joining them*). How can you tell?—it's so dark.

EMILY. There's only a little moon, but enough to see by. Look—there he goes—back into the wood.

LAVINIA. Poor Papa—poor dear Papa—he'll never see a squirrel again.

HARRIET. Don't, Lavinia. (*She sits on the upstage seat* C.)

JANE. Do you think he would wish to?—(*She sits on the downstage seat* C.) I mean—not to see any more squirrels is surely one of the lesser disadvantages of dying.

(BURROWS *enters.*)

BURROWS. You rang, Mr. Jasper?

(EMILY *sits in the armchair* R.C.)

JASPER (*going up to* BURROWS). We are ready for the box now, Burrows.

BURROWS. Every one of them, Mr. Jasper—regulated to the minute—I did them myself.

JASPER. Not the clocks, Burrows, the box.

BURROWS. I had a mort of trouble with the one in the library—it struck fifteen three times—but I fixed it. (*He gives a slight cackle and then controls himself, then he moves to the door.*)

JASPER. The box, Burrows—we want the box—I told you to have it brought down from the attic this morning.

BURROWS. Oh, the trunk! Very well, Mr. Jasper.

(*He goes off.*)

(JASPER *crosses to the fire.* HARRIET *rises and goes to sit at* L. *end of the couch.*)

LAVINIA. It seems callous somehow—so soon to pry upon Papa's secrets.

JASPER. Callous perhaps, but certainly necessary.

JANE. I observed one of his more open secrets at the back of church this morning.

LAVINIA. What do you mean, Jane?

JANE. Mrs. Wynant.

HARRIET. That creature.

JASPER. Hush, Harriet—we cannot resent her grieving too—in her own way.

HARRIET. Nevertheless, I do resent it.

LAVINIA. She should not have come.

EMILY. Poor Mrs. Wynant.

LAVINIA. Really, Emily—poor Mrs. Wynant indeed!

EMILY. I was thinking of the Will.

RICHARD. It was perfectly just—she had no claim.

JASPER. No legal claim, at any rate.

LAVINIA. Jasper!

JASPER. It would be unchristian to deny her a certain moral right.

CHARLES. Moral is hardly the word I should have chosen.

JASPER. Spoken like a soldier, Charles—and also, I'm afraid, like a gentleman.

(BURROWS enters.)

BURROWS. The box is outside, Mr. Jasper—if you and Mr. Richard—I would rather Martin did not enter——

JANE. Why, Burrows, it really wouldn't matter.

BURROWS (*coming down to* JANE). It isn't the clatter, Ma'am, it's his face, it's so very hot and red—in this pale room—you understand?

JASPER. Very well, Burrows—come along, Richard.

(RICHARD and JASPER go out—JASPER behind the sofa.)

BURROWS. Will there be any tea required, Ma'am?

JANE. Yes, please, Burrows—a little later.

BURROWS (*cupping his ear with his hand*). I beg your pardon, Ma'am?

JANE (*shouting*). A little later, Burrows.

BURROWS (*respectfully*). Oh no, Ma'am—certainly not—not for the world, Ma'am.

(BURROWS *goes out.*)

JANE. What could he have thought I said?

CHARLES. I fear that we shall never know.

(RICHARD *and* JASPER *return with a very dusty little trunk. They put it down down stage* L.C.)

JASPER. Sarah has done her best with a duster, but I fear it needs scrubbing.

RICHARD. Never mind.

LAVINIA. The box.

HARRIET. Oh, dear—the box.

(*She comes down* L. EMILY *comes down* R. *of the box,* EDWARD *up* R. *of it.*)

JASPER. Yes, there it sits—reproaching us—almost frowning at us.

JANE (*standing*). Those little straps make it look even more disagreeable than it really is.

JASPER. You have the key, Lavinia. You took it from Father's chain.

LAVINIA Yes, it's here. (*She hands it to* JASPER.) You're the eldest.

JASPER. Before opening it—before unearthing our dear Father's secrets—I must most earnestly enjoin—complete discretion.

CHARLES. Of course.

JASPER. You, Charles, and Edward, and my dear Jane——

JANE. Open it, Jasper.

JASPER. You cut me short, Jane, in the most frivolous way.

JANE. Never mind.

CHARLES. We understand, Jasper—complete discretion.

JANE (*impatiently*). Open it!

JASPER (*on his knees*). Poor Papa! (*He wrestles with the lock.*) The key doesn't fit—— (*He lifts the lid.*) It's already open—— (*He puts his hand into the box and produces a gilt paper crown.*) It's the wrong box!

LAVINIA. Oh, how stupid of Burrows!

(*All gather round the box.*)

EMILY. A paper crown.

HARRIET. I remember it.

RICHARD. Where's the sceptre—there should be a sceptre too—I made it myself from Uncle William's walking-stick—— (*He searches in the box, kneeling.*)

EMILY. He was very angry.

RICHARD (*finding it*). Here it is.

LAVINIA. There was a scarf with beads on it from India—I wore it when I was the Queen—— (*She goes on her knees too, and searches in the box.*)

HARRIET. And there were four swords—flat ones—but one was broken—— (*She joins* LAVINIA *and searches in the box.*)

EMILY (*kneeling beside the others*). Princes and Princesses—— Oh, how lovely!

JANE. What on earth are you talking about?

JASPER (*smiling*). Princes and Princesses—it was a dressing-up game—we played it when we were children——

HARRIET. On Sundays—only on Sundays——

(*They sing a foolish little tune. During it* EMILY *and* HARRIET *go to the couch with* LAVINIA. RICHARD *and* JASPER *fight up* C. CHARLES *goes up* L., EDWARD *up* R. JANE *sits in the chair down* L.)

"PRINCES AND PRINCESSES"

EMILY. Princes and Princesses
              Every rainy day
          In our party dresses
              Made a trifle gay
          With a rose and shawl,
              We would act a play
          In the servants' hall.

> Lavvy was the evil Queen,
>   Wickeder than Nero,
> Jasper, being just thirteen,
>   Always played the hero.
> Crown and sceptre,
>   Rose and ring,
>   Magic charms for everything,
> Death, destruction, fire and flame
> Was our Sunday game.

(Dance.)

ALL.   Princes and Princesses
>   Every rainy day,
> In our party dresses
>   Made a trifle gay
> With a rose and shawl,
>   We would act a play
> In the servants' hall.

LAVINIA (*at the fireplace*). This is wicked—wicked—I shall never forgive myself to the end of my days——

(*The others look at her mutely.* RICHARD *rises from the floor where he has been lying since being killed in the duel, and dusts himself down.*)

JASPER (*crossing to* LAVINIA). Don't cry, Lavvy—please don't.

(EMILY *is on the couch, and* HARRIET R. *of it.*)

LAVINIA (*tearfully*). God must surely punish us for this heartlessness, dancing and singing and playing, with Father not yet cold in his grave.

JASPER (*crossing to the table* R.C.). That is an emotional statement, my dear, understandable in the circumstances, but hardly accurate.

EMILY. The cemetery really is very exposed, Lavinia.

LAVINIA. Forgive us, Papa, forgive us——

RICHARD (*crossing* C.). A little more Madeira, Jasper, our sister is becoming hysterical.

(JASPER *pours out some Madeira and hands it to* RICHARD,
who takes it to LAVINIA.)

Here, my dear.

LAVINIA. No, no—I don't want it.

JASPER. Drink it, Lavinia, it will calm you.

JANE. I think I should like a little more, too. (*She
crosses to the table.*)

CHARLES (*pouring it for her*). Very well.—Harriet?

HARRIET. Yes, please. (*She crosses to the table, then
up* C.)

JASPER (*to* LAVINIA). Come along, dear.

LAVINIA (*sipping the wine*). How shameful—— Oh,
how shameful!

CHARLES. Emily, some more wine?

EMILY (*rising*). May I, Edward?

EDWARD. Yes, my love, but only a little. (*He is
down* R.)

CHARLES. There is only a little left.

RICHARD. We had better ring for some more.

LAVINIA. No, Richard, no—I forbid it.

RICHARD. As you say, Lavvy, but my throat is
cruelly dry.

CHARLES (*crossing* C.). Mine, too.—Jasper?

JASPER. Dry as dust.

LAVINIA (*bursting into tears again*). Dust! Oh,
Jasper!

(*The door opens discreetly and* BURROWS *enters bearing
another decanter of Madeira. Everyone looks at him
in silence as he places it ceremoniously on the tray.
He looks inquiringly at* CHARLES *who is holding the
empty decanter.* CHARLES *gives it to him. He bows
politely and goes to the door. He turns and regards
them all lovingly for a moment then, from his cuff, he
produces a large white handkerchief with which he wipes
his eyes, but it is difficult to tell whether he is laughing
or weeping. He goes out, closing the door behind him.*)

JASPER (*moving up* C.). With every advancing year
Burrows grows wiser.

HARRIET. And kinder.

RICHARD. And more understanding.

JASPER. Surely, among ourselves, a little private toast to Burrows would not be entirely without grace ?

CHARLES. Hear, hear !

LAVINIA. Papa would not have approved at all——

EMILY. I think Papa would have wished it.

EDWARD. Well spoken, my love.

LAVINIA (*crossing to the table*). Jasper—I appeal to you——

CHARLES. What harm is there, Lavinia ?

(*The men go to the drink table.* RICHARD *then crosses back* L.)

JANE. Don't be silly, Lavinia.

JASPER. The " Ayes " have it—charge your glasses.

(*Everybody refills their glasses.*)

(*Raising his glass.*) To Burrows—our first friend— Don't you remember, Lavinia ? He made us toys in the woodshed. He read us stories when we were ill ; he gave us forbidden sweets from the pantry. He loved us all—you particularly, Lavinia. Have you forgotten his tenderness when Mother died ? Have you forgotten his welcoming smile when we came home from school ? Surely this small gesture of affection to him can only be a pale sin in the eyes of heaven. To Burrows, Lavinia.

LAVINIA. To Burrows ! (*She drinks.*)

ALL. To Burrows !

(*They drink.*)

CHARLES. That was delicious.

RICHARD. I think it must have come from Papa's special cellar.

EMILY. I believe I should like a little more.

(JANE *and* JASPER *put down their glasses on the table.*)

EDWARD. No, Emily.

EMILY (*gaily*). Spoilsport—I defy you !

(She quickly pours herself out another glassful and drinks it before anyone can stop her.)

HARRIET. Emily!

LAVINIA. Behave, Emily.

JASPER. You shock me appallingly, Emily; I'm almost sure you do.

EDWARD. I apologize, Jasper—I apologize to you all. *(Going to* EMILY.*)* Come to bed, Emily.

EMILY. Papa liked wine—he liked it to excess—I expect this is hereditary. *(She giggles.)*

EDWARD. Come to bed immediately.

EMILY. I shall do no such thing, my love, so there! I want to see what more there is in the box—— *(She kneels on the floor beside it and begins to rummage about in it.)*

LAVINIA *(up L. of the couch)*. I feel a little faint—the heat, I think, and everyone behaving so strangely

HARRIET *(going to her)*. My dear——

JANE *(going to* LAVINIA*)*. Would you like me to take you upstairs?

LAVINIA. No, no, it will pass—it's nothing.

RICHARD. Some salts—some vinegar?

LAVINIA. No, no—I think perhaps a thimbleful more of that wine——

CHARLES *(pouring her out some)*. Here, my dear——

LAVINIA. Thank you, Charles—how kind. *(She accepts it weakly.)*

JANE. I feel a little strange myself.

JASPER *(upstage of couch)*. Beloved!

HARRIET. Charles, open the window.

JANE. No—the air is damp—it would be dangerous.

RICHARD. Some wine?

JANE. Perhaps—perhaps that would revive me. *(She goes to the table.)*

(RICHARD, EDWARD *and* HARRIET *are up* L.)

CHARLES *(pouring her out some)*. Here, my dear.

JANE *(smiling gaily)*. Thank you, Charles.

EMILY (*at the box*). Oh, look—look——!

JASPER. What is it?

EMILY. The musical box—don't you remember?

RICHARD. I thought it had dropped to pieces years ago.

LAVINIA. Aunt Heathcote gave it to us—it was a Christmas present.

(JASPER *kneels by the box.*)

HARRIET. Papa forbade us to play it.

EMILY (*taking it to the table and winding it*). He can't forbid us now!

EDWARD (*reprovingly*). Emily!

EMILY. Shh! Be still—listen——

(*They all listen—no sound comes from the musical box.*)

JASPER. It's old and tired, it's forgotten how to play.

RICHARD. No, no—there was a little catch—I'm sure there was——

EMILY. Make it play, Richard—please try——

(RICHARD *tinkers with it and it strikes one note. They all sing* "Let's play a tune on the music box." *They stop singing and the musical box tinkles out a tinny little melody. They sing.*)

ALL. Let's play a tune on the music box,
Let's play a tune on the music box.

(*Then it plays again.*)

RICHARD. There!

EMILY (*clasping her hands ecstatically*). Oh, how sweet —how sweet!

HARRIET. The red schoolroom curtains, blowing out in the draught—I can suddenly see them——

RICHARD. The hard pink sugar on the edge of the cake—I can suddenly taste it.

JASPER. Your hand in mine, Jane, when you were brought over to tea by your governess—I can suddenly feel it.

JANE. Oh, darling!

" Music Box "

JASPER.	Let the angels guide you,
RICHARD.	Be good and brave and true,
CHARLES.	Let the angels guide you,
EDWARD.	Oh do—Oh do—Oh do!

LADIES.   Let the angels guide you,
               Be good and brave and true,
               Let the angels guide you,
               Oh do—Oh do—Oh do!

JANE.   Spurn each vile temptation,
               Avoid each evil lure,

JASPER.   Keep your conversation
               Inordinately pure.

EMILY.   Lift your hearts to heaven
               And pray for ultimate grace,

ALL.   Be always virtuous just—in—case!

(JANE *crosses* R. *then moves about among them.* EMILY
and EDWARD *sit on column seat.* HARRIET *sits on couch.*
LAVINIA *sits on armchair down* L. JASPER *sits downstage seat* C.)

JANE   But of course, in this vale of tears
               Life may sometimes cheat a bit.
               Hearts are prone to beat a bit,
               Causing great confusion.
               When temptation to sin appears,
               Try to be discreet a bit,
               Look well before the leaping,
               Dream true awake or sleeping,
               Love tears are waste of weeping,
               Let reason override you—guide you.

ALL.   Look well before the leaping,
               Dream true awake or sleeping,
               Love tears are waste of weeping,
               Let reason be your guiding star.

JASPER.   Jane, I'm surprised, I'm ashamed of you,
               Such a material point of view.

JANE (*spoken*). Nonsense, Jasper—I was voicing your
own beliefs—you taught them to me.

JASPER.   True—very true ! (*Singing.*)
            Keep your soul's endeavour
            Sufficiently sincere,
            Purity is ever
            An excellent veneer,
            Good may be rewarded
            In some indefinite place,
ALL.   Be always virtuous just—in—case !
HARRIET. There was another tune as well—I
remember distinctly—it played another tune——

(EMILY *takes another drink.*)

RICHARD. We mustn't ask too much of it.
JASPER. Try the little catch again, Richard.
HARRIET. It was a waltz.

(*They all talk.*)

JANE (*looking at* JASPER). Of course it was—a waltz
—don't you recall it, my dear love ? We danced to it
years later—at a ball—just before we were married—
it was this—it was this——

(*She starts to sing* " Hearts and Flowers." RICHARD *is
still at work on the music box—suddenly it begins to
play again—the tune that* JANE *is singing.*)

" HEARTS AND FLOWERS "

JANE.   Hearts and flowers,
Dreaming hours
Under skies of blue,
Two fond hearts so sweetly beat ⸢EMILY. It's remem-
      in tune,   bered ! Oh, how
'Neath the midnight magic of the⎜ clever of it.
      moon ;   RICHARD.   Hush,
Petals falling,   Emily ! That was
Love-birds softly calling,   ⸤ their love-song.
Life begins anew
When Cupid's dart discloses
The secret of the roses,
Hearts and Flowers and You.

JASPER (*spoken*). The man who wrote those words certainly had a sweet tooth.

HARRIET. I remember Annie singing that song when she was doing the stairs.

LAVINIA. I remember Nanny singing it when she was bathing Emily.

RICHARD. I remember father humming it between his teeth when he was whacking me with his slipper.

CHARLES. An excellent example of two hearts beating to the tune.

JASPER. A crude joke, Charles. Back to the barrack-room!

JANE (*smiling*). We found it inspiring enough, did we not, Jasper?

JASPER. Olympian, my dear—the loveliest song in the world.

(JASPER *and* JANE *sing to each other the love song of their youth. The others join in, humming very softly, as they dance together.* JANE *and* JASPER *cross* R. LAVINIA *rises.* RICHARD *stands between her and* HARRIET.)

BOTH (*singing*). Hearts and Flowers,
        Bygone hours,
        How the time has flown.
JASPER. You wore white camellias in your hair;
JANE. All you did was hold my hand and stare!
BOTH. Have we altered?
        Have our footsteps faltered
        Through the years we've known?
        When all our days are done, love,
        There'll still be only one love,
        You and you alone.

(*At the end of it,* JANE *sinks to the floor in a deep curtsy;* JASPER *bows over her, taking her hand.*)

JASPER. For ever, my heart.
JANE. 'Till death us do part——

(*He raises her to her feet and takes her in his arms,* LAVINIA *sinks on to the couch once more in tears.*)

RICHARD. Oh, Lavvy!

JASPER. Don't cry, Lavinia.

LAVINIA. Don't mock me—these are true tears.

(JANE *crosses to* LAVINIA.)

JASPER. Not sad ones though, I beg of you—

LAVINIA. Mama died when we were little, Papa died four days ago, but life isn't dead, is it—is it?

JASPER. Never, as long as it's gay, as long as it's happy.

EMILY. Poor Papa—poor dear Papa!

LAVINIA. To hell with Papa! (*She rises.*)

HARRIET. Lavinia!

RICHARD. Lavinia!

EMILY. Oh, Lavvy, how can you!

JASPER. Bravo, Lavvy!

LAVINIA. I mean it—give me some more Madeira, Charles.

CHARLES. Good heavens!

LAVINIA. I hated Papa, so did you, Jasper, and Harriet, and Richard and Emily——

EMILY. Oh, Lavvy—don't—don't——

LAVINIA. He was cruel to Mama, he was unkind to us, he was profligate and pompous and worse still, he was mean——

CHARLES (*handing her some wine*). Here, my dear—drink this.

LAVINIA (*taking it*). Certainly I will—— (*She raises her glass.*) Now I will propose a toast—to Papa—and to the truth, too—Papa and the truth together—for the first time.

JASPER. I do hope you will not regret this in the morning, Lavinia.

HARRIET. Don't you think you had better retire to bed?

EMILY. I feel frightened.

LAVINIA. This may be wicked. (*Going to* EMILY.) I expect it is—I expect I shall be punished for it—but I don't care. You escaped—all of you—you found husbands and wives and lives of your own—but I had to

stay here—with him—— For years he has scarcely
spoken to me—I've counted the linen—(*crosses down* R.)
I've added up the bills—I've managed the house—years
ago I said good-bye to someone I loved because my
miserable, unkind conscience told me that it was my
duty. I've sat here in this house week after week,
month after month, year after year, while he insulted
me and glowered at me and betrayed our name with
common village loves. (*Down* C.) The Will—the happy
Will which was read to us to-day was made ten years
ago—you realize that, do you not?

JASPER. Lavinia——

LAVINIA. What you do not realize is that he made
another—a week before he died——

HARRIET. What are you saying?

RICHARD. Lavinia—are you mad?

EMILY (*wailing*). Oh, Lavvy!

LAVINIA. None of us were even mentioned in it.
Five thousand pounds was left to Mrs. Wynant. Six
thousand pounds to Rose Dalton. Three thousand
pounds to Mrs. Waterbury—I can only gather that
she was less satisfactory than the others—and the rest
to a fund for the erection of a new church containing a
memorial of himself in black marble!

JASPER. Lavinia—are you sure of this?

LAVINIA. Quite sure. (*In front of the couch, turning
to* JASPER.) Burrows witnessed it.

JASPER. And would it be trespassing too far on your
indiscretion to ask what became of it?

LAVINIA. Seven and a half minutes after Papa
breathed his last, Burrows and I burnt it. (*She sits
at* L. *end of the couch.*)

(*They all sigh.*)

JASPER (*crossing to the window*). Ring the bell,
Richard.

(HARRIET *sits in the chair down* L. JANE *at* R. *end of
the couch.*)

RICHARD. Very well. (*He goes to the bell and pulls it.*)

JANE.   Black marble—how very nasty.

RICHARD.   Black clay would have been more appropriate.

(CHARLES *refills their glasses.*)

EMILY.   Poor Mrs. Waterbury.

JANE.   Think of the humiliation she has been spared.

HARRIET.   I wonder where Rose Dalton is now ?

JASPER.   In Scotland, I believe—she married a Baptist.

EDWARD.   Do you suppose Mrs. Wynant suspects ?

JASPER.   Suspects what, Edward ?

EDWARD.   About the—er—about your father—about what Lavinia has just told us ?

LAVINIA.   I observed an expensive diamond brooch fastening her cloak in church to-day. That, I think, should be a sufficient reward for services rendered.

JASPER.   How hard you are, Lavinia.

JANE.   And how right.

(BURROWS *enters.*)

BURROWS.   You rang, Mr. Jasper ?

JASPER.   Yes, Burrows.

RICHARD (R. *of the couch*).   We wish to ask you a question, Burrows.

BURROWS.   Much better, thank you, Master Richard. A little herb tea soothes all disharmony.

JASPER (*crossing to* BURROWS).   A question, Burrows.

BURROWS.   Very well, Mr. Jasper.

JASPER.   Miss Lavinia gives me to understand that you witnessed my late father's last Will and Testament.

BURROWS (*cupping his ear with his hand*).   I beg your pardon, sir ?

JASPER.   Did you or did you not witness my late father's last Will and Testament ?

BURROWS.   My affliction is increasing bad, Mr. Jasper, I shall never be able to hear that particular question.

LAVINIA (*softly*).   Thank you, Burrows.

BURROWS.   Not at all, Miss Lavinia.

JASPER. Some Madeira, Burrows ? (*He holds up the decanter.*)

BURROWS. I should be honoured, Master Jasper.

JASPER (*pouring him some*). Here, then.

BURROWS (*accepting it*). At your service always.

JASPER. Thank you, Burrows.

BURROWS (*catching sight of the musical box*). Have I your permission for a moment ?

JASPER. Certainly—what is it ?

BURROWS. There should be a little tune (*kneels by the box*) a little tune from the years that are dead—allow me——

(*He starts the musical box. It plays the same gay little melody that it played before. He stands beside it, bending down to hear it more clearly, then he stands up with his head nodding to the tune, and raises his glass.*)

I drink to you all—— (*Then to* JASPER *and* JANE.) And to you, Sir, and Ma'am—this house was happy when there were children in it—— (*He drinks.*)

They all drink. EMILY *and* JANE *and* HARRIET *start to sing "* Let the Angels Guide You." *All the others join in. The tune becomes gayer and swifter until they are all hand in hand and dancing round* BURROWS *as—*

The CURTAIN *falls.*

FURNITURE AND PROPERTY PLOT

FURNITURE

Linoleum.
2 armchairs.
1 pr. little chairs.
Low chair.
Chair.
2 footstools.
Corner shelf what-not.
Fire-screen.
Wire flower-pot stand.
Column stand.
Circular padded seat—round column.
Mantelpiece.
Two-shelved table (Canterbury).
Long fire stool.
Square fruit-topped table.
Work-basket table.
Round lacquer table.
Cushion on S-shaped seat.
Long narrow table.

PROPERTIES

Stage R.
 Carpet.
 Picture of sailing boat.
 Woman's portrait.

In Flower Stand.
 Fern centre.
 Down Stage.—Aspidistra.
  Red flower.
 Up Stage.—Purple flower.
  Pencil head of man.
  On corner shelved what-not.

Descending.
 China framed mirror.
 Ornament.
 Ornament and glass shoe.
 Jug.

34

On Alcove.
  Draped statue of girl.
  Portrait of man.
  Venetian blinds, lace curtains.
  Lace pelmet.

Stage L.
  Portrait of woman.

In Alcove.
  " Venus of Milo."

On Column Stand.
  Blue beau pot, containing pampas grass.
  Flower picture.
  Picture of woman and two children.

On Mantelpiece.
  Cover.
  2 glass drop ornaments.
  Clock centre.
  Large portrait of woman.

On Two-Shelved Table.
  Above.--Gold wooden framed picture.
             China King Charles dog.
             Small blue vase.
  Below.--Music.
             Picture of dog.

Under Cushion on Couch.
  Purse with key in.
  Bell pull.

In Backing.
  On Table.—China vase.
               Print of old man.
               Oval print.

Off Stage R.
  2 lace tray-cloths on trays.
  10 Madeira glasses and small decanter on one.
  Large decanter on the other.
  Black trunk with 2 straps and padlock.

In Trunk.
  Golden paper crown.
  Toy sceptre.
  4 wooden swords (one broken).
  Shawl.
  Musical box.
  Rose.
  Rug bottom of trunk.

Off Stage L.
  Clock chime.

FAMILY ALBUM

A Victorian Comedy with Music

by

NOEL COWARD

PLAYED IN "TO-NIGHT AT 8.30"

SAMUEL FRENCH

LONDON
NEW YORK   TORONTO   SYDNEY   HOLLYWOOD

822coω 29862

FAMILY ALBUM

822 lou

29862